ABORTION!

GEORGE AND GIOVANNA

CAROLYN BOOKER-PIERCE

J Merrill Publishing, Inc., Columbus 43207
www.JMerrill.pub

Copyright © 2021 J Merrill Publishing, Inc.
All rights reserved. No part of this publication may be reproduced, distributed, or transmitted in any form or by any means, including photocopying, recording, or other electronic or mechanical methods, without the prior written permission of the publisher, except in the case of brief quotations embodied in critical reviews and certain other noncommercial uses permitted by copyright law. For permission requests, contact J Merrill Publishing, Inc., 434 Hillpine Drive, Columbus, OH 43207
Published 2021

Library of Congress Control Number: 2021909793
ISBN-13: 978-1-954414-00-6 (Paperback)
ISBN-13: 978-1-950719-99-0 (eBook)

Title: Abortion!: George and Giovanna
Author: Carolyn Booker-Pierce

CONTENTS

Introduction	v
1. Giovanna's Questions Answered	1
2. George's Questions Answered	15
3. I Know I Am Forgiven	23
4. The Grace of God	29
5. When He Restored My Soul	35
6. Making Better Choices	43
7. Naming My Children	47
8. A Word to The Fathers	55
9. Receiving Forgiveness and Healing	59
10. God Will Finish What He Started	63
Definitions	71
About the Author	73
Also by Carolyn Booker-Pierce	75

INTRODUCTION

I dedicate this book to George and Giovanna, my two children whose lives I chose to abort by giving my consent. While it is hard to acknowledge, this is a part of my life I had to face responsibility for and accept the consequences. My two children are not here.

During that time in the 1970s, I was faced with two powerful influences. The first one was my dad. I truly believed he loved me; however, when I got pregnant for the first time at 16 years of age, he stopped speaking to me. Not that he talked a lot in the first place, but the look he had on his face after my mother told him of my pregnancy I will never forget.

Introduction

It was a look of such disappointment and anger at the same time. That went on for the remainder of my pregnancy. It was my goal to avoid him at all costs.

Because my father did not have any words for me, he did seem to voice his disapproval to my mother. Bless her heart. She got to hear all his likes and dislikes when it came to his children.

I remember wanting to visit a family member, me and another sibling that was pregnant. He made it clear how ashamed and embarrassed he was and how we did not need to accompany him to the family member's house.

That was the first time I felt the horrible sting of being shamed for my teenaged pregnancy. It was from my father.

It was not until my child was born that my father came around. He saw this adorable baby boy who melted his heart. He was looking into the eyes of his first grandchild.

My father no longer had that look of shame and disapproval. That first grandchild stole his heart and became a person he truly loved until the day he died.

Introduction

It was amazing to see how a man who had been hell-bent on not engaging in the birth of my child become so soft and kind. However, the shame that was sown would stay with me for years.

After that experience, I did not want to ever have another child out of wedlock. That became my mission in life.

Not even two years later, I was pregnant again.

Still, in my teenage years, I was adjusting to raising my child as a single mother and succeeding in it. Another pregnancy? What will I do now?

I was still living in my parent's home. I had not forgotten the reaction from the first pregnancy. My thoughts were, I could not be a disappointment and bring shame to my father again.

During that time, there was a lot about abortion being an alternative to pregnancy. Planned Parenthood was advertising on television along with their offer of birth control pills. The information I received turned out not to be completely true but enough that I bought into the idea. I will talk more about that in my answers to George and Giovanna.

Introduction

While I gave my consent, you will find it was out of my immature reaction as a young, confused, and ignorant person. I didn't know enough about abortion.

Knowing what I know now by no means excuses the choices I made. I made the wrong choice not once but twice. That does not make me a bad person, neither does it make you a bad person if you have chosen to abort a child/ren.

One thing I want to make clear, this is not a book about pro-life or pro-choice. This book is about the choices I made that I later regretted. It is also not a book of judgment. I am not God. I don't know what God's plan was for you or your child/ren.

You may have been in a life-or-death situation and had to have an abortion. That is not my business. That is between you and God. However, in my case, I feel I made the wrong choice twice.

If it speaks to you in the same way, so be it. It is about my journey of forgiveness and healing. I needed to move on from the guilt and shame I was personally experiencing. I felt a need to be forgiven not by man or others but by God and my children.

Introduction

I have already asked God the Father to forgive me. I have prayed and asked George and Giovanna for forgiveness. I believe I have received that forgiveness from God, George, and Giovanna, my two aborted children. In the word of God according to 1 John 1:9;

> *If we confess our sins, he is faithful and just to forgive us our sins, and to cleanse us from all unrighteousness.*

That is why I believe I am forgiven. I have confessed that I have done something wrong that interfered with the birth of my two children. Because my two children's spirits still live and will rise when Jesus Christ the Messiah returns, they have his spirit. Therefore they were not born into sin. They will have the same Spirit of the almighty God. The God who forgives and has no sin in Him.

I want those who read this book to know I am writing with a humble heart. A heart that still breaks and heals when I think about or share this story: I believe sharing my story is necessary. By sharing my experience of aborting my two innocent children, George and Giovanna, I hope that someone will know my truth about abortion, forgiveness, and healing.

Introduction

I understand it is not everyone's truth, but it is my truth as a believer in Christ. I hope I can help stop another mother like myself from making the same unnecessary choice. I didn't have to commit the same mistake.

While I am writing this book, I pray that Holy Spirit will guide me in what to say, not to offend anyone but bring glory to God and healing to the reader. Despite my choices in abortions, I hope to help bring the same forgiveness and freedom God offered me when I asked him to forgive me to others.

I hope to help heal the hearts and minds of someone filled with the guilt and shame resulting from their choice of abortion. I hope that someone who may be thinking about aborting their unborn child will consider other options.

It is my hope the word of God will comfort those who read this book by meditating and reflecting on the words found in Romans 8:1-2,

> *There is therefore now no condemnation to them which are in Christ Jesus, who walk not after the flesh, but after the Spirit. For the law of the Spirit of life in Christ Jesus hath made me free from the law of sin and death."*

Introduction

Therefore, if you have acknowledged that abortion is not the right thing to do for you and repent, asking God for forgiveness (which means turning away from abortion and walking in the Spirit which gives life, there is no condemnation), you can walk away from your past mistakes or current mistakes and be forgiven. You can be encouraged to know, especially when you have messed up not once, but twice and maybe three times like myself Philippians 1:6 says,

> *Being confident of this very thing, that he which hath begun a good work in you will perform it until the day of Jesus Christ.*

Thank God he will finish what he started in you and what he has begun in me. God did not change his mind about you, and he did not change his mind about me. God knew what choices you and I would make and how they would be paid. He sent Jesus Christ the Messiah to die for and pay for our sins.

> *For this is my blood of the new testament, which is shed for many for the remission of sins*
>
> — Matthew 26:28

1
GIOVANNA'S QUESTIONS ANSWERED

For we all have sinned and, come short the glory of God.

— ROMANS 3:23

How could you do this to me? Giovanna may have asked.

Giovanna, this is the story that lead me to make my decision to abort you.

It was the summer of 1975. I was that eighteen-year-old that thought I knew everything.

Looking back now, I realize I knew nothing. I was already a mother of a beautiful child around eight months old. I had dropped out of high school around age sixteen, and I became pregnant not long after.

I already started working at a daycare right after I had quit high school. Then I had started working a different job at a recreation center. I thought no one would notice my pregnancy. I worked alone in an office at a neighborhood recreation center. I only interacted with those picking up and turning in gym equipment.

I ended up having to quit working when my stomach started getting too big to hide. Of course, they did not want to risk something happening to me while working there.

I went home for the rest of the summer to wait on the birth of my first child. At the time of the delivery of my first child, I had turn seventeen.

I could not go back to work for a couple of years due to my child struggling with asthma. We spent a lot of time at the local Children's Hospital. There were times we were at the hospital all night long. He was even admitted at one point.

We spent so much time at the hospital I had begun to know all the doctors on the third shift by name. The asthma attacks would seem to always happen late at night.

Abortion!

In the year 1975, my self-esteem was low. I felt like I could not accomplish much of anything. My only goal and concern had become taking good care of my son and making sure he was alright. I hated myself but not my child, who was my only source of motivation.

During the early summer of 1975, I started dating a military guy. I will call Airman. Airman had a great personality and was very friendly. I tend to be drawn to outgoing, extroverted men due to my natural bend as an introvert. Those who know me now may not see me as an introvert, depending on how close I am to them. I am a licensed social worker, marriage and family counselor, and I work in ministry. So at times, I can seem very outgoing.

At the beginning of our short-lived relationship, Airman was very nice to me and those around. He was very loving and kind to my son. The relationship was good until drugs became an issue and began to influence Airman's behavior.

The more involved he became with drugs, the more Airman's personality began to change. I confess I did smoke weed during that time. However, his behavior became that of irritation and aggression. Just before things got bad with

Airman and me, I was pregnant again at eighteen years old.

Did I mention I was seventeen giving birth to my first?

I had no job. I could not work. I had no plans for my life, let alone the life of my first child, other than to survive. The thought of bringing another child into the world, unmarried, unemployed, feeling there was no future with Airman was frightening.

What was even more frightening was revisiting that look on my father's face again. That look of shame and embarrassment I did not think I could handle.

I was beyond scared, embarrassed, and ashamed. I allowed my fear and shame to get the best of me. The thought that came to mind "Abortion."

And may I point out during that time, it seemed common. It was a lot of talk about abortion in the 70s. It appeared common at the time. Many were using abortion as an answer to unwanted pregnancies. It was a voice only a few would dare to talk about if it involved them.

Abortion!

I see it now as a voice straight from the enemy called Satan. I did not know that voice back then, but I know it now. Satan knew I was scared, embarrassed, and ashamed.

He knew I did not know, based on the information I was receiving, that it was the wrong information for me. I listened to that voice because of ignorance regarding the false information being put out about abortion. I didn't know the facts, and it seemed like a good idea at the time.

Keep in mind at 18 years old, in the 1970s, my knowledge concerning abortion was very limited. The information that I have now I did not have then. The abortion clinics and Plan Parenthood were a bunch of liars and deceivers. They only cared about their funding and passing out birth control pills. Put all that together, and you have the reasons that lead me to abort you.

The information I was given during the 1970s was not all true.

It was said abortions were legal. That part was true. Then came the lie.

The lie that helped persuade my choice to abort you, Giovanna. I was told you were "just a fetus." You were not a human or a baby yet. The information I was given back then was, you were just tissue in my body, not a formed child. That information was anything but the truth. Years later, I found out you were a live human being with a heart beating living inside of me.

Since abortion was "legal" and I was worldly, my understanding of abortion was warped and diluted. It was easy to say yes to the voice in my head. So, off to the clinic, Airman and I went. Like two dumb sheep taking our child to the slaughter.

I remember there was not much said. I don't remember Airman offering any alternatives or suggestions. He seemed to just go along with the choice of the intelligent person that I was (I was not smart at all). Yes, I am being sarcastic.

He only had a blank look on his face, but he never said anything that I can remember. Neither of us had much to say.

We arrive at the clinic. I was led away to a room with an upright table with white sheet covers, a nurse, and a doctor who hardly said anything. Both were ready to work on me like they were working on an old car removing a part with no substance, feeling, or meaning. I do not remember the doctor even speaking. He seemed cold and impersonal. I was scared half to death and wondering why this "legal" choice I was making was starting to feel wrong and illegal.

During the procedure, something inside of me did not feel right at all. It was very uncomfortable physically, but I thought, "I am not killing a baby, but this sure feels wrong?"

Now I know that you, Giovanna, were a live human being, a person, with a spirit and a life. The spirit inside of me was not in agreement with what had I had agreed to do, abort you.

Despite not being a born-again believer at the time, I still had a feeling deep down inside of me signaling something is wrong. I just didn't know how to respond to the feelings at the time. If I knew what I know now, I would be like Forrest Gump, "Run, Forrest, run."

While reading my Bible one morning, I got my answer to why I was able to feel something was wrong. Romans Chapter 2:14-15 TMLB: The Maximized Living Bible:

> *Those who are not Jews (unbelievers) do not have the law, but when they freely do what the law commands, they are the law for themselves. This is true even though they do not have the law. They show that in their hearts they know what is right and wrong, just as the law commands. And they show this by their conscience. Sometimes their thoughts tell them they did wrong, and sometimes their thoughts tell them they did right. (My emphases)*

My conscience, which is my inner thoughts, was warning me. Something was wrong. You know that check in your spirit or sometimes discernment. Even though I was not a born-again Christian like the Jews, Paul was speaking of in Romans. I knew in my heart the feelings of right and wrong. I did not know the Bible and had nothing in writing to say it was wrong, but my conscience was speaking through my carnal mind trying to tell me something was wrong.

When I asked for further information about the termination of my pregnancy, I will never forget what a licensed nurse told me, and I am sure many others were told during that time: "You are not terminating a baby. You are terminating a fetus.

The fetus is not a baby because it has not developed yet."

That day, I put my trust in a nurse that I thought was telling me the truth, only to find out years later it was a lie. That day, I aborted you, Giovanna, and terminated your life. While I was told you were only a fetus, you were more than just a fetus.

You were alive and well until the point of termination. You were a live baby that, no matter how small and how underdeveloped you were, you were a baby, my baby.

I allowed a doctor I trusted to kill you, to terminate your life. Yes, I gave my permission to a licensed professional to kill you, my baby. Thank God there is so much more education and information on pro-life and abortion today than it was back in the 1970s.

Airman and I were young, and least to say ignorant. We didn't know when we pulled up at the clinic the seriousness of what we were about to do.

However, there was a quietness that suggested something was wrong. We left the clinic that day, saying nothing. I went and laid down for the rest of the day like I was told. The next day my body began to restore itself physically but deep down inside my spirit, in my heart, was a void left from me terminating of you. Giovanna that I did not fully understand.

I was experiencing the death of a child that I could not properly grieve because I did not know the extent of what had happened. There had been a murder, and I did not realize it neither did I want to know it.

I would have given birth to my baby if I had known the truth and had been spiritually minded and not carnal. Even though some people are born-again believers, they still have chosen to have abortions.

The world tells us it is okay to be pro-choice. Yes, abortion is our choice, but we must understand the choice being made. We can behave like unbelievers with no conviction when we walk in our flesh. Please know that I am not judging any Christians who had an abortion because *we all have sinned and come short of the glory of God*, according to Romans 3:23.

> *If we say that we have no sin, we deceive ourselves, and the truth is not in us.*
>
> — 1 John 1:18

Therefore, we all can thank God for His forgiveness, mercy, and grace, when we repent and ask for forgiveness. We can all thank God for godly sorrow that can lead us to repentance. I will discuss this more in Chapter 10.

I am saying it is not enough just to be a born-again Christian. Christians who believe in Christ, the savior, are capable of sin. However, we must learn to be more spiritual (God-conscious), not carnal (natural, worldly), in order to receive what our conscience is telling our spirit concerning what is right and wrong.

> "But the natural man recieveth not the things of the Spirit of God: for they are foolishness unto him: neither can he know them, because they are spiritually discerned.
>
> — 1 Corinthians 2:14

In summary, I was a young, ashamed, high school dropout already with a child out of wedlock to answer Giovanna. I was afraid of giving birth to another child out of wedlock, and marriage was not an option with Airman, who would soon be assigned somewhere else in another state.

I was not told the truth concerning what it meant to abort a baby (fetus). It was only by the grace of God the child I already had was being cared for. I was a stay-at-home mother unable to work for the first couple of years of his life due to his health condition.

Lastly, I was carnal in my thinking, not hardly the Christian I am today. I am not perfect, but I am better. My morals and values have changed in a big way since those days in the 70s. However, I needed God back then, and I need him now.

I did not realize how much I needed God then. God would have helped me as he did with my first child. I did not understand how much grace was given to me. God would have helped you too. God would have forgiven me for having another child out of wedlock.

While there are consequences to our choices, God does not judge us like man. Therefore, I trust God that has forgiven me now. I asked Him to forgive me. Now, Giovanna, I am asking you to forgive me as well. Thank you for forgiving me.

I will one day see you in heaven. I can hardly wait. Until then, I know the Father in heaven is taking good care of you. Now enjoy your better life until I see you on the side. Love Mom.

2
GEORGE'S QUESTIONS ANSWERED

George, since I believe you are a boy, I will cut to the chase. It was in the dead of winter, February 1978. I remember the month and the year because a lot had transpired that year.

I remember finding out I was pregnant again by a childhood friend. Your father and I had crossed paths at the job we were both working at. I worked the day shift. He was working the evening shift. When I was leaving to go home from work, he was coming in to work.

I had not seen him in years. We were excited to meet up after not seeing each other, from little children to adults. I was surprised he recognized me first.

We dated for several months. After a couple of months in, I noticed your father had a problem with alcohol. At first, I thought he was experimenting like many of us young folk did. However, alcoholism was like a family curse, as several of his family members indulged in alcohol.

It became more and more apparent to me that I needed to get out of the relationship. I didn't need to be in another unhealthy relationship. I was slowly trying to ease my way out of the relationship. I didn't think he would take me dumping him very well. When he did drink alcohol, he would become easily angered, and I was honestly afraid of his reactions.

Well, just when I had built up the nerve to get out, I got sick. I couldn't believe it. Not again, I was pregnant with the man's child I was trying to leave. Yes, George, I was running from your father. Honestly, I felt having you would have kept me tied to your father, which I knew couldn't happen.

I thought my only way out again was to do the wrong thing again. I ran back to the abortion clinic. I don't even remember if I told him. I remember one of my friends from work took me.

Abortion!

The same week of the abortion, my childhood home caught fire. I lost everything I had worked for and was proud of. I had just started to be more responsible, so I thought. I was buying things in hopes of moving out of my parent's home.

I was taking care of the only child I had given birth to. He seemed to be thriving and adjusting well in the life I brought him into. I was just in a relationship with a man I knew again I had no future.

I was pregnant again, back at the abortion clinic, and the house had caught fire. Again, I was being told the same thing I was told with your sister's abortion. "It is not a baby. It's only a fetus." That was again to say you did not exist as a human yet. There I was with the same bad feelings, but this time it was worst.

I remember crying as a grieving mother that had just lost her child. The problem was I had made that choice without understanding the severity of my choice. I could not have cried harder at a funeral.

I realize now that the spirit of God in me was crying out of my spirit. It was trying to tell me I was doing the wrong thing. It was so much worst than the first time with Giovanna.

With Giovanna, it was a sadness I did not understand. This time it was sadness and the guilty feeling of doing something terribly wrong. I sensed I was losing someone that should be here alive. You, George.

I sensed I should have been giving birth, not aborting. Even though I thought you, again, like Giovanna, were "just a fetus." I felt strongly that I did something wrong.

After that horrible experience being so painful, I did what I should have done back in 1975 before the first abortion with Giovanna. I started reading books about the process of birth and fetal development.

While it was too late for you and Giovanna, it was not too late years later. I read about every stage a baby is developed, from week to week and month to month. It was then that I realized I had not killed one but two live babies, you and Giovanna.

I am truly sorry because I realize what I had done and could not change it. Again, I found myself needing forgiveness. Therefore, I had to ask God and you for forgiveness. I know I didn't deserve it, but I did not know and understand the truth about abortion until years later.

My choice to abort you and Giovanna was wrong. It was a horrible time for me. I do not think I would have survived the effects of aborting you, the shame, the house fire, and that impending breakup if it had not been for the good that happened that same year in April 1978.

Several months after the last abortion, depression came. I felt like the biggest failure; hopeless and numb. However, I still knew it was up to me to change things if things were going to get better.

At first, I didn't know how to change. I was still trying to plan my way out of the relationship with your father. I had very little strength and confidence in myself. The planning was just a thought. I did not have the energy or will to put it into action.

I was drowning in despair. I knew I needed something to happen and that my life could not remain the way it was. I needed something greater than myself to motivate me to make some positive changes, like getting out of the unhealthy relationship and making better choices.

. . .

In April 1978, I attended a friend's wedding shower. I showed up only because she asked and I did not want to tell her no. I did not want to be there.

I arrived at the church where the wedding shower was held. I was trying to interact, but this spirit of sadness had overtaken me. It was something that I had never experienced that heavy before, especially on what should have been a joyful occasion.

Out of nowhere, at the most inappropriate time, I started crying uncontrollably. I learned later it was a spirit of conviction all over me. Another friend came up to me to see if I was alright. I was not about to explain how bad my life was at that time, but she could tell I needed prayer. She and another friend invited me up from the basement of the church into the church sanctuary.

There they prayed for me and led me in what is called the sinner's prayer of forgiveness. That day I accepted Christ as my personal savior. That day I became a born-again believer in Christ. That day I experienced freedom from all the guilt and shame I had been carrying for the last couple of months. All the guilt and shame from aborting you,

Abortion!

George, and the shame I had tried to bury from aborting Giovanna. Yes, me, the person that had no hope for her future, got saved. I was born again. In John chapter 3 verse 3 it states,

> *Jesus answered and said unto him, Verily, verily, I say unto thee, Except a man be born again he cannot see the kingdom of God.*

I could now see the kingdom of God. That kingdom was full of righteousness, joy, and peace through his Son, Jesus Christ, Yeshua, the Messiah, because I was now born again. That wonderful day in April 1978, my life changed. I finally had hope for my future. I started attending the church where God saved me. I found out more good news through prayer and Bible Study. This wonderful scripture,

> *Therefore if any man be in Christ, he is a new creature: old things are passed away; behold, all things are become new*
>
> — 2 Corinthians 5:17

Just the thought of my old life becoming new was good news. It gave me the strength I needed to leave that unhealthy relationship. It helped me look forward to all things becoming new. I moved on from making the old kind of mistakes, like abortion. I had a new hope that I would see you, George, and your sister, Giovanna, again in heaven.

Unfortunately, George, your father passed away several years later. He was still young; therefore, I assume it was due to his struggle with alcoholism. It is my hope he was able to make the same commitment that changed my life. That commitment to Christ granted me forgiveness of my wrong choices and the many sins I had committed, especially your abortion. That same forgiveness was available to him. My hope is I will see you and Giovanna when I get to heaven and even your father. I love you, George. I wish I had made a better choice, but I didn't. Thank you for forgiving me. Love mom.

3

I KNOW I AM FORGIVEN

If we confess our sins, he is faithful and just to forgive us our sins, and to cleanse us from all unrighteousness.

— 1 JOHN 1:9

It was not long after I had accepted Jesus Christ as my Lord and savior that I knew I was forgiven. In my new life of prayer and meditation time, I would read my Bible and pray. Then it was like a light bulb would come on in my heart and mind as I read the scriptures. I was hungry to know more about God and his forgiveness through his Son, Jesus Christ, Yeshua, the Messiah.

Holy Spirit was teaching me then as he does now how I should live. Holy Spirit would shine a light on the truth in God's word as I read it. That truth, in God's word, was setting me free. Until that point, before my salvation experience, I had been carrying around this massive weight of sin and guilt on my shoulders.

However, the more I read the word of God, the freer I became. The word of God taught me that Christ died on a cross so my sins could be forgiven. Not only that, I was predestined to be a child of God, despite my past mistakes. I knew I was forgiven when I read scriptures like the following,

> *Having predestinated us unto the adoption of children by Jesus Christ to himself, according to the good pleasure of his will, 6 To the praise of the glory of his grace, wherein he hath made us accepted in the beloved. 7 In whom we have redemption through his blood, the forgiveness of sins, according to the riches of his grace;*
>
> — *Ephesians 1:5-7*

It was all in God's plan for me to be forgiven. It was in His plan for me to be adopted as his child. He sent Christ to die on a cross so that my sins would be forgiven and the world can experience that same forgiveness. John 3:16 is still just as powerful today as it was when I heard this gospel of love and forgiveness back in April 1978,

> *For God so loved the world, that he gave his only begotten Son, that whosoever believeth in him should not perish, but have everlasting life.*

I deserved death for what I did to Giovanna and George. But God offered me everlasting life; what a blessing to know that after everything I had done in aborting George and Giovanna, I could still be forgiven and living a life everlasting free of sin.

Again, this is not to bring guilt or judgment to anyone who has had an abortion. Your circumstances may have been different than mine. What I do know is the good news. We all can have the same forgiveness after having had an abortion or guilty of other sins. That means to repent and tell God you are sorry, then turn from doing that sinful thing again. As I continued to read, Holy Spirit would lead me to this type of message when the enemy (the devil) would try to bring up my past,

> *There is therefore now no condemnation to them which are in Christ Jesus, who walk not after the flesh, but after the Spirit. 2 For the law of the Spirit of life in Christ Jesus hath made me free from the law of sin and death*
>
> — ROMANS 8:1-2

I no longer had to walk in the shame and condemnation that I had put on like old clothes after abortion. Abortion was most certainly the wrong decision that I had made. However, I did not have to walk around wearing the clothes of shame any longer. That garment no larger fit me because *there is therefore now no condemnation*. I dropped that garment and put on new clothes called the spirit of truth. In Ephesians chapter six, the new clothes I now wear as truth are a part of the armor of God for my protection,

> *Wherefore take unto you the whole armour of God, that ye may be able to withstand in the evil day, and having done all, to stand. 14 Stand therefore, having your loins girt about with truth (v.13-14a).*

I came to know that by confessing my sins, *he is faithful and just to forgive us our sins,* and God takes

Abortion!

it a step further. He is so good he will, *cleanse us from all unrighteousness (1John 1:9)*

Now I am free from the guilt and shame of abortion. Now I am free to move on with my life without that burden hanging over me. There is nothing like having a clear conscience after doing something you feel in your heart is wrong. After confessing, not hiding my sin, I was free to ask for forgiveness and let others know they could be free. Why?

> *If the Son therefore shall make you free, ye shall be free indeed.*
>
> — *John 8:36*

I am free because I am forgiven. How do I know I am forgiven? Because the Bible says the Son has made me free and I am forgiven in first John 1:9. When did I know I was forgiven? When I confess my sins, according to first John 1:9, I was forgiven. Thank God for sending his Son to die for our sins. He took care of my sins and yours on the cross once for all.

> *For Christ also suffered for sins once for all time, the just for the unjust, so that He might bring us to God,*

CAROLYN BOOKER-PIERCE

— 1 Peter 3:18a NASB

4
THE GRACE OF GOD

For by grace are ye saved through faith; and that not of yourselves: it is the gift of God:

— Ephesians 2:8

I want to start this chapter by saying that by no means is this book written to justify any abortions that I have had or that you have had unnecessarily. It is my conviction that abortion is a serious offense against unborn children. Abortion is something that I am now totally against practicing or doing.

Again, this is my story and my conviction. I am not God, judge, or have a right to judge anyone who has had or plan to have an abortion. I just know my take on abortion now that I know the truth. My truth is aborting a living child no matter how many weeks in the pregnancy is not ideal. Some may say they are carrying a child that may come out deformed, or the doctor has told them to abort for that reason. I would reference what God said to Moses when he complained about his handicap of speech,

> *And the Lord said unto him (Moses), Who hath made man's mouth? or who maketh the dumb, or deaf, or the seeing, or the blind? have not I the Lord?*
>
> *— Exodus 4:11*

God knew Moses had a speech problem when he was in his mother's womb, but God still had a plan for Moses. God planned to use Moses' voice to free the children of Israel from 400 hundred years of slavery with his voice. After Moses went to Pharaoh several times, telling him with his voice to let God's people go and after God sent many plagues to Pharaoh. It happened. Pharaoh sent for Moses,

> *And he called for Moses and Aaron by night, and said, Rise up, and get you forth from among my*

people, both ye and the children of Israel; and go, serve the Lord, **as ye have said**

Exodus 12:31

What if Moses had not been born when God needed to send him to help free slaves. They may have continued to be slaves. But God did not care about Moses' condition. He had a plan for Moses, just like he had a plan for every child he creates. I now believe it is not my choice to decide who will live and who will die. Again, this is not to condemn anyone, including me.

However, I hope to help bring a different perspective about choosing life over abortion for a disabled unborn child. The grace of God can help us overcome and do anything.

I would only ask, what is your heart saying after you have spoken to God in prayer about abortion? Now to move on regarding the grace of God. The grace of God is an amazing gift given to those of us who do not deserve to receive it. The Merriam-Webster dictionary has several definitions for grace. That is how powerful grace is. You can't sum it up in a couple of words, but here are a few I pulled from Merriam-Webster,

- Unmerited divine assistance is given to humans for their regeneration of sanctification
- A virtue coming from God
- A state of sanctification enjoyed through divine assistance
- Approval, favor stayed in his good graces
- Lastly, mercy and pardon

The first words in the definition of the word grace are described as unmerited divine assistance given to humans for their regeneration. Unmerited means *not adequately earned or deserved: not* <u>*merited*</u>. To put that in a sentence, I would say, "God's grace or divine assistance is something I did not adequately earn or deserve to be given." While I needed to be regenerated meaning, *spiritually reborn, or converted*, I did nothing to merit that restoration *to a better, higher, or more worthy state.* And the last part of the first definition of grace, *sanctification*. Meaning I did not deserve *the state of growing in divine grace as a result of Christian commitment after baptism or conversion,* being born again. However, God allowed me to be a partaker of his marvelous grace, *unmerited divine assistance given to humans* (like you and me) *for their regeneration or sanctification.*

Abortion!

Simply put, I did not deserve the grace of God, his favor, or his forgiveness. If it were not for the grace of God, where would I be? After two abortions, where would I be if had not his unmerited favor upon me? I know where I would probably be. I would be somewhere still wearing the filthy clothes of guilt and shame. I would be somewhere not knowing how to be set free after abortion. I would be somewhere not being able to forgive myself and others the way God has forgiven me and others. I thank God for his grace that I don't deserve.

I will never forget that there is nothing good enough I could ever do that could merit his grace and favor. I must always remember what the scripture says about grace,

> *For by grace are ye saved through faith; and that not of yourselves: it is the gift of God;* [9] *Not of works, lest any man should boast.*
>
> — EPHESIANS 2:8-9

Grace is a gift. It is by grace through faith that I am a born-again believer who is set free from sin. It is only by his grace through your faith that you and I will be free from sin. Please accept the gift of God's grace and forgiveness today! Ask for forgiveness and enjoy the blessing of God's grace. The grace that none of us who has had an abortion or contemplating deserves. Grace is a freely given gift from God. However, you must accept it. Do you accept the gift of grace that saves you from your past today? Do you accept the gift of grace that could save your life and the future life of an unborn child?

Just think, it was nothing but the grace of God that saved celebrities like Apple's Steve Jobs from abortion; Oprah's mother was encouraged to abort but chose not to, and Brooke Shields, whose grandfather paid her mother to abort her, but her mother couldn't do it. Reverend Jesse Jackson Jr was **conceived out of statutory rape; his mother, a 16-year-old student, was pressured to abort him, but she chose not to.** Many famous people would not have been here if their parents had decided to abort them. Please check out the complete stories of these amazing people and others in the article of those who were almost aborted, *Welcome to the Truth, Pro-Life Survivors - 23 Celebrities Almost Aborted* as their stories are told? https://welcometotruth.com/blogs/apologetics/pro-life.

5

WHEN HE RESTORED MY SOUL

He restoreth my soul: he leadeth me in the paths of righteousness for his name's sake.

— Psalms 23:3

In this chapter, I will be interchanging the word soul with the word mind. The soul is your mind, will, and emotions. Part of experiencing the grace of God that we talked about in the last chapter is we experience restoration of our soul (mind).

After having multiple abortions and before receiving forgiveness, I had a hole in my soul. My mind needed to be healed, but I was not sure how to heal it. My soul was out of source, not connected to the right source, which was God. My soul was separated from its lifeline. That is what mistakes and sin does. It separates you from God.

When I made my connection with God, I received forgiveness. I not only received forgiveness, but I also received restoration. I needed restoration for my traumatized heart and mind that was affected due to the distorted choices I made to abort not once but twice.

The act of abortion left me wounded emotionally and mentally. When I chose abortions, I tried not to think about what I had done. However, buried in the back of my mind, carried the brokenness of what I had done—leaving my soul wounded and broken.

However, God restored me to my original innocent state with love and peace of mind. Whereas I am no longer considered guilty. Our hearts and minds can become restored to having a loving relationship with ourselves, with God, and even with the child/ren, we chose to abort. Merriam Webster's definition of restore,

1. give back, return
2. to put or bring back into existence or use
3. to bring back to or put back into a former or original state: renew

4. to put again in possession of something

During the time I was making a choice to abort, I lost myself. You can almost say I lost my mind. I later realized that I was not in a good and healthy relationship with myself, God, or the children I aborted. I was disconnected from my heart and needed to be mentally, spiritually, and emotionally restored in all these areas. I had cut myself off from the loving-kindness I needed and deserved from God and myself as a human being.

I would have made better choices if I loved myself and if I had loved God. Most of all, my unborn children.

To love them, I had to first see them as in human forms. My relationship with myself and God needed to be restored and renewed by renewing my mind (Romans 12:1-2). My mindset and relationship to having unplanned children needed to be restored in my mind.

I needed a new perspective. I needed to start giving back to myself the love and kindness I had lost over my impressionable years. Then I could have loved others better, including my unborn children.

Me not having a relationship with the God of love made it difficult for me to love myself. I did not understand I was loveable before making the wrong decisions of abortion and afterward. I thought God did not love me because of the choices I was making before and after abortion.

You see, God never left me or cut me off "*Never will I leave you; never will I forsake you*" (Hebrews 11:13). The problem was I never let him in. I thought I had to be perfect in order to be loved, saved, and restored by God. Only to find out that it was only by the grace of God alone I could be loved, saved, and restored. Remember the free gift,

> *For by grace are ye saved through faith; and that not of yourselves: it is the gift of God* [9] *Not of works, lest any man should boast*
>
> — (EPHESIANS 2:8-9

Once I understood that God loved me and died for all the foolish mistakes I made back then and now, I could love and forgive myself. I was able to allow the restoration process to begin. Not that God gave me a license to sin, but He gave me forgiveness for sin.

Abortion!

For this is my blood of the new testament, which is shed for many for the remission of sins

— MATTHEW 26:28

Restoration is what I needed after being disconnected from God and myself for most of my younger days. Merriam Webster's definition of restoration,

> 1: an act of restoring or the condition of being restored: such as
> a: a bringing back to a former position or condition: reinstatement the restoration of peace

I needed restoration first with my relationship with the God who made me and then with myself. After the restoration of my mind, I heard and discerned more clearly right and wrong. I started making better decisions because I had a better relationship with God, who began to guide me as I listened to him.

I knew even after abortion that God was still on my side, willing to *lead me in the path of righteousness for his name sake Psalms 23:3b.* However, my mind had to be restored to its original state. My soul needed to be healed. I needed to be put back into my former position with the God I had run away from. God restoring my mind gave me the peace I needed to carry on in life after abortions. The better life I needed after making some of the worst mistakes of my life.

I have learned I no longer have to live a life full of guilt and shame because of abortion. I can be forgiven and restored. The good news is you can be forgiven and restored too. You can be restored and live with a peaceful mind after abortion. Please understand I am not promoting or judging abortion? I am saying as a witness what happened to me once I allowed God to restore my mind (soul).

Some people believe God would not restore childbearing after abortion. That is not true. Several years later, after I learned the truth about abortion, I gave birth to another son. I am so glad that I got the revelation on abortion, or one of the apples of my eyes would not have been born.

You see, I did not plan him either, but what I now understand, he was in God's plan. He and his brother are the pride of my life, as well as George

Abortion!

and Giovanna. I have four beautiful children and a bonus child. I can't wait to see them all together in heaven. That is where we all will meet.

If you want to see your aborted child/ren, ask God for forgiveness and ask him to come into your life and restore you like he did for me. He will not only restore your mind; he will restore your life. All you need to do is ask.

You may think it is too late; the children I gave birth to are nine years apart. Read the scriptures so that you can see all the promises of God on restoring and restoration. He is willing and able to restore all the years that were stolen from you due to your choices before renewing your mind and knowing what the scripture says. Here is one of those promises,

> *And I will restore to you the years that the locust hath eaten, the cankerworm, and the caterpillar, and the palmerworm, my great army which I sent among you.*
>
> *— Joel 2:25*

Sometimes God will allow us to go through things until we turn to him for guidance, forgiveness, and restoration. Sometimes that thing he allows is abortion. I still make mistakes based on my mind's misinformation but thank God he is still restoring and renewing my mind (soul) today. Why not let him restore your soul today?

6

MAKING BETTER CHOICES

I call heaven and earth to record this day against you, that I have set before you life and death, blessing and cursing: therefore choose life, that both thou and thy seed may live:

— *Deuteronomy 30:19*

Today you and I both have another chance to make a better choice. God has given us another opportunity to choose life when it comes to having children. We have the option to choose life or death. God encourages us to choose life so that our children, our seed, can live.

This is not just about aborting the seed of our children. What about aborting other seeds God has planted that we deem as unplanned events?

Take, for instance, a situation or opportunity that comes up that you did not plan, so you canceled that plan because it didn't happen in the time frame you wanted. You killed the plan. You start saying things like, "It is not the right time," or "I don't have the money," or "I am too old to do that."

Sometimes, we need to learn how to make better choices and trust God. That may take understanding the plan and the will of God. That may take you reading the word of God and praying for guidance and instructions. Sometimes we think it is just us that is bringing something or someone into our path.

Remember I said earlier, I had another child after abortions. It was not a thoroughly thought-out planned pregnancy. What I mean by that is I wanted another child. However, the timing wasn't right.

If I did not know the word of God and the truth about abortion by that time, I would have chosen wrong again. My amazing son would have found his fate with the other two children I aborted. Thank God I chose right that time.

Abortion!

I chose life so that my son could live. God did not have to give me another chance. The first pregnancy, I chose life; the second and third, I chose death; and the fourth, I chose life. I had a choice every time.

God did not go against my will; however, I suffered for not choosing life. The two babies suffered because I did not choose life. They did not live. While I am forgiven, it would have been a shame if I continued choosing death after knowing that God wanted me to choose life.

After knowing the truth about abortion, I know my choice to abort affected the lives of two others. They did not get to choose. I chose for them. I have a whole new perspective on making choices today than I did years ago, especially when I think about how my choices will affect another. Life is precious. It is a gift from God, no matter the timing, no matter the circumstance or the child's condition. Life is a gift.

> *Lo, children are an heritage of the Lord: and the fruit of the womb is his reward.*
>
> — PSALMS 127:3

7

NAMING MY CHILDREN

Once I started to understand what took place in the early weeks of pregnancy, such as a baby having a heartbeat within the first 5 to 6 weeks after gestation. I understood that both of my children were living, breathing human beings. They both had taken the form of who they were to become. God had planned them both before they entered my belly.

> *Before I formed thee in the belly I knew thee; and before thou camest forth out of the womb I sanctified thee, and I ordained thee a prophet unto the nations*
>
> *— JEREMIAH 1:5*

It became more personal and harder to accept the reality of what I had done. However, I excepted my wrongdoings, and I excepted my forgiveness as well. Yes, I could have continued to waddle in the fact that I gave permission to abort two children, but I wanted to move to something that gave me joy and peace.

The first thing that gave me joy was the knowledge I would see my children again. You may be asking how you will see them again? I am glad you asked. You will only understand what I am about to say if you believe in the word of God. As I began to read more of God's word, I began discerning that God was speaking to me that I will see my children because they died in him. The following passage of scripture confirmed that for me.

> *For the Lord himself shall descend from heaven with a shout, with the voice of the archangel, and with the trump of God:* ***and the dead in Christ shall rise first***
>
> — *1 Thessalonians 4:16*

The two children I aborted were innocent and died in God. Innocent babies that had their life taken from them by the sin I committed.

Abortion!

Therefore, God did not punish them; he rescued them, so they will rise first when Christ comes back again. I will see them because of my choice to believe in Christ, the savior. If you have had a child/ren, you aborted, they will rise first. You can see them too if you are a believer *in Christ* heaven bound.

> *For the Lord himself shall descend from heaven with a shout, with the voice of the archangel, and with the trump of God:* **and the dead in Christ shall rise first:** [17] **Then we which are alive and remain shall be caught up together with them in the clouds, to meet the Lord in the air: and so shall we ever be with the Lord.**
>
> — 1 Thessalonians 4:16-17

If I die, I will rise with them. If I am alive when Christ comes back, I will *be caught up together with them in the clouds.* How exciting it was and is to know I will see my children. Now concerning the names of my children. Understanding they were not just a fetus; they were my children, I felt a need to name them.

I started seeing these visions of a girl and a boy. Therefore, I came up with the name George for the boy and Giovanna for the girl. It didn't happen in a moment. I took some time looking up names and their meanings just like I would do if they had been born here on earth. I had named my sons I had given birth to after their fathers. Why not do the same for my other son? I always wanted a girl. It came back to my memory. I always liked Italian names like Giovanny, so I found the name Giovanna for my daughter. So, I named my daughter Giovanna. See the meaning of her name below.

Meaning of "Giovanna"

> Italian name; Other origins for the name Giovanna include - Italian, Hebrew. The name Giovanna is most often used as a girl name or female name. In Italian, the name Giovanna means - God is gracious.

I like the meaning of Giovanna's name. It speaks of God being gracious. If you remember, we talked about the grace of God being his unmerited favor. Most of all, giving me what I don't deserve, like forgiveness.

Abortion!

Like I have already shared, I named George after his father, who is now deceased. See the meaning of his name below.

Meaning of "George"

> Other origins for the name George include - English, Greek. The name George is most often used as a boy name or male name. In English, the name George means Farmer. In medieval legend, St. George: (the knight who became the patron saint of England) struggled with a fire-breathing dragon symbolizing the devil.

Did you see the meaning of George's name? It means farmer. A farmer sows and reaps. Saint George was a Christian. Saint George struggled with the enemy (the devil) for Christians. I love it. He was a soldier. I can't wait to see my children. I believe that God gave me those names. Because one represents God's grace and the other represents God's salvation that God made available to us all (John 3:13)

Sure, I choose their name, but I had no idea what their names meant until I looked them up. That confirmed their names for me. See more on Saint George below.

> ***Saint George*** *(*<u>*Greek*</u>*: Γεώργιος; died 23 April 303), also* ***George of Lydda****, was a* <u>*Christian*</u> *who is accepted as a* <u>*saint*</u> *in* <u>*Christianity*</u>*. According to traditional rumors, he was a soldier in the* <u>*Roman army*</u>*. His parents were Christians of Greek origin. His father, Gerontius, was a* <u>*Cappadocian*</u> *serving in the Roman army. His mother, Polychronia, was a Christian from the city of* <u>*Lod*</u> *in Palestine. Saint George was a soldier of* <u>*Cappadocian Greek*</u> *origins, member of the* <u>*Praetorian Guard*</u> *for* <u>*Roman emperor*</u> <u>*Diocletian*</u>*, who was sentenced to death for refusing to recant his Christian faith. He became one of the most* <u>*venerated*</u> *saints and* <u>*megalomartyrs*</u> *in Christianity, and he has been especially*

Abortion!

> *venerated as a <u>military saint</u> since the <u>Crusades</u>.*

Naming my children turned out to be a spiritual experience that was very healing and a sign of God's love, forgiveness, and mercy towards my aborted children and me. He loves them, and he loves me. God loves you, and he loves any of your children that may have been aborted. Try it. Pray and ask God to help you name your children. If you are a born-again believer, you will see them, **and the dead in Christ shall rise first** <u>1 Thessalonians 4:16</u>.

Don't you want to see your children? Believe in the Lord, and you will be saved and see your children.

> *And they said, Believe on the Lord Jesus Christ, and thou shalt be saved, and thy house*
>
> — ACTS 16:31

That means you and your family. Do you believe? I will talk more about this in the next chapter. Right now, just think about naming your child/ren. It is healing and freeing. Naming my children helped healed me and gave me peace and a connection that was not there.

8

A WORD TO THE FATHERS

Since I was not the only one involved in producing a child, I feel I need to address the fathers of aborted children, not in a condemning way but honestly. I am sure that some fathers out there were present or knew about their unborn children that were aborted. I know in at least one case, the father knew and took me to the abortion clinic.

Fathers usually don't say a lot in general. I don't see them having much to say when it comes to abortion. Women are generally good at reminding men and the rest of the world, "it is their body." I am sure there was still, in fact, a man willing to speak up but did not stand a chance if he protested abortion. On the other hand, some men will speak up when trying to get rid of a child and encourage abortion.

Men keep many things to themselves and just don't talk about them most of the time. Abortion isn't something most people want to rehearse or bring up as normal conversation; however, the fathers have just a much responsibility for the unborn child's conception, especially if they know about it.

There should also be some forgiveness and healing in their hearts for their aborted child or children. If the father knew about the abortion, he might be experiencing the same guilt and shame as the mother. Therefore, the same forgiveness available to the mother of her aborted child/ren is available to the father if he chooses to ask for forgiveness.

Those that have spiritual and moral values like I do now but did not have at the time of my abortions tend to feel more shame and guilt due to the offense. Participating in an abortion is almost like you going with another person to commit a crime. While you may not be the person who pulls out the gun or pulls the trigger, you can be guilty by association due to driving the car or being present. Everyone involved is charged with the offense. You participated by accompanying the mother of your child to the clinic, or you knew about the abortion.

While I understand that a man has no control over a women's body, if that were the case, the men in my life would have had more to say over the choices I made with my body. They did not. Therefore, fathers are not solely responsible but may have some guilt over the abortion of a child.

There could be some real feelings hidden and buried that were never dealt with up until now. I want every father who has lost a child to abortion to be free of guilt by first acknowledging that it was a real child lost—then asking for the same forgiveness that God freely gives when we ask. Then accept your healing. Sometimes that one act will change things in your heart forever. Remember, if you are a born-again believer, you will see that child again whether you want to or not. You don't want to be caught off guard. The child will rise again, *and the dead in Christ shall rise first:* (1 Thessalonians 4:16b).

9

RECEIVING FORGIVENESS AND HEALING

He healeth the broken in heart, and bindeth up their wounds.

— PSALMS 147:3

When I first understood the magnitude of what I had done in aborting George and Giovanna, my heart was broken. It grieved me that I caused their lives to end before they could begin. I cried and was sadden over their lives that were destroyed. God knows if I had known better, I most likely would have chosen better.

I believe that I would have chosen better because once I knew the truth about abortion, I never aborted another child. Abortion left a terrible ache in my heart that I tried to bury, but once the truth about abortion was revealed to me, I could no longer suppress it.

I thought that hurt might be there forever. However, in the same year, I mentioned earlier in 1978 of the last abortion, I had the wonderful experience of meeting my savior and healer. I was introduced to my Father, the Lord Jesus Christ, and asked for forgiveness of my sins. That is when forgiveness and healing began to take place. When I accepted Christ as my savior, not only I began to heal from the pain of abortion, but healing began for other things I had done wrong in my life.

During that time, I learned how much God loved me, and he loved the world. I was learning God had sent his only son to die for my sins so I would not have to pay a debt I could never repay. Think about the worst thing you have ever done. God is willing to forgive you of that thing if you repent, say I am sorry, and stop doing that thing you did. There is healing in knowing you can be forgiven for all the wrong you have done, even abortion. All of this by believing in God as your savior and asking him to forgive you.

For God so loved the world, that he gave his only begotten Son, that whosoever believeth in him should not perish, but have everlasting life.

— John 3:16

You may still be thinking that God the Father could never forgive you if you have had an abortion and other horrible things. However, the last I checked, the only sin that is not forgivable is the sin of blasphemy against the Holy Ghost, written in the book of Mark.

But he that shall blaspheme against the Holy Ghost hath never forgiveness, but is in danger of eternal damnation

— Mark 3:9.

Thank God, we who Christ has redeemed by his grace can receive forgiveness for every sin and mistake we have made.

In whom we have redemption through his blood, the forgiveness of sins, according to the riches of his grace;

— Ephesians 1:7

10

GOD WILL FINISH WHAT HE STARTED

Being confident of this very thing, that he which hath begun a good work in you will perform it until the day of Jesus Christ

— PHILIPPIANS 1:6

This book was the most challenging book I have ever written. The good news is that God gave me the grace to write it. He does not waste anything. What God started in me like this book he is finishing. I was supposed to write this book.

There was a time I thought I would never finish. I hope that in writing this book, someone will be blessed by the content.

We have all made bad choices in our life. We will all continue to make bad choices here and there. That is all a part of being human.

While it is not an excuse for bad behavior, it the truth. It is essential to know that God will finish what he started in us despite our choices, good or bad.

You may be thinking you have messed up so much, especially if you have had an abortion. You may think that God can't use you or bless you. However, there are a lot of things that we as humans start and feel can't be finished because of what we have done. That is not always true.

If God starts something in us that he wants us to finish, he will finish it. Look at me. If you are reading this book, that means I finished it.

***

In my earlier years, I thought life couldn't get any worst for me. Those were the days I needed God the most, and he showed up for me.

God is not like man. He does not bolt on us because we have done some wrong things in our life. If that were the case, many of us would never succeed or have a relationship with God. God has always had a plan of good and not of evil (Jeremiah 29:11) to give us a hope and a future. Therefore, he is faithful who promised us even when we don't always do the right thing. He didn't change his mind about us because his love is everlasting.

> *The Lord hath appeared of old unto me, saying, Yea, I have loved thee with an everlasting love: therefore with loving-kindness have I drawn thee.*
>
> *— JEREMIAH 31:3*

God loves you even if you have had an abortion. I know you may be suffering from guilt and shame. Here are some suggestions you can do to help you with your forgiveness and healing.

1) Repent (turn away from doing what is wrong). Admit that you have done something wrong. Ask God to forgive you, and he will; according to 1 John 1:9,

If we confess our sins, he is faithful and just to forgive us our sins, and to cleanse us from all unrighteousness.

2) Confess and believe that he is Lord and able to save. He will; according to Romans 10:9-10,

That if thou shalt confess with thy mouth the Lord Jesus, and shalt believe in thine heart that God hath raised him from the dead, thou shalt be saved. [10] For with the heart man believeth unto righteousness; and with the mouth confession is made unto salvation.

3) Let God forgive, heal and restore you. Start by saying the following prayer based on Romans 10: 9-10,

> *Father I confess that I have sinned against you. Now I repent of my all my sins because you word says, "for all have sinned, and come short of the glory of God;" (Romans 3:23). I also confess you as my Lord and savior. I invite you to come into my life and live in my heart. I believe in my heart that you died on the cross for my sins and God raised you from the dead so that I could be saved. With my heart I believe you have made me righteousness. My confession has now led me to salvation. I thank you for forgiving me, cleansing me and saving me. I believe and I receive you as my savior. In Jesus Name. Amen!*

Just that simple. Now read the scriptures like John, Romans, and Psalm. Pray that God will continue to heal you and lead you to a Bible-believing church.

Tell someone about your choice you made in prayer. That is true confession.

4) Forgive yourself. If God is willing to forgive you, why are you still holding on to unforgiveness? Read Romans 8:1,

There is therefore now no condemnation to them which are in Christ Jesus, who walk not after the flesh, but after the Spirit.

5) Ask your aborted child/ren to forgive you. That will help set your mind free.

6) Believe God will restore and heal your soul (mind). Psalm 23:3

7) Name your children. That will help you to accept they were real lives even if they are not here right now.

8) Know that you can see your child/ren in heaven, if you have made the above prayer and confession. 1 Thessalonians 4:16-17 see above

9) Seek professional help or spiritual counseling, if you suffered from depression or any other mental health issues resulting from abortion.

Where no counsel is, the people fall: but in the multitude of counsellors there is safety. Proverbs 11:14

10) Remember, there is nothing in your life that can't be forgiven except for blasphemy against the Holy Spirit.

> *And so I tell you, every kind of sin and slander can be forgiven, but blasphemy against the Spirit will not be forgiven. ^{32} Anyone who speaks a word against the Son of Man will be forgiven, but anyone who speaks against the Holy Spirit will not be forgiven, either in this age or in the age to come*
>
> — MATTHEW 12:31-32

Remember, *if we confess our sin, he is faithful and just to forgive us our sins, and to cleanse us from all unrighteousness* (1 John 1:9). You know when you have a big ugly stain on your clothes that look dirty. You want to clean that stain immediately. Once the stain is cleaned, it is no longer there.

That is the way God wants to forgive and cleanse you. While you know the stain was there, you can no longer see it, and no one else can see it because it has been removed. God will finish what he started.

I know everyone reading this book has not had an abortion. Some may be just reading out of curiosity. However, you may know someone who has had an abortion. If so, please share so they can be forgiven, restored, and healed. I hope you have enjoyed my story.

I look forward to seeing George and Giovanna when we all get together in heaven. I know they are great kids. Every one God has made and created he called good.

> *27 So God created man in his own image, in the image of God created he him; male and female created he them.*
>
> *31 And God saw every thing that he had made, and, behold, it was very good.*
>
> — Genesis 1:27, 31a

You see, everything that God has made is very good. Therefore, it does not matter about the timing, birth effects, and your part in the child's existence. God made every child that was created born or unborn and said it was good.

I have noticed some of the most beautiful children are children with disabilities. It is okay if you don't feel equipped to handing the challenged. There are people in the world prepared and ready to adopt those beautiful children every day. As far as I am concerned, adoption is better than abortion. That is my opinion.

If you are pregnant and thinking about abortion, you may want to try other options. There may be another way for you to choose. I'm just saying; I am sure George and Giovanna would agree. I am praying this book has been a blessing to someone who has had an abortion/s.

Again, I am not here to judge anyone. You have just read my story. I have totally put my business in the street about abortion in this book. You are not alone if you have. Don't forget there is forgiveness, restoration and healing, and a guilt-free life after abortion. Blessings!

DEFINITIONS

Grace Definition,
https://www.merriam-webster.com/dictionary/grace

Unmerited Definition,
https://www.merriam-webster.com/dictionary/unmerited

Restore Definition
https://www.merriam-webster.com/dictionary/restore

Restoration Definition
https://www.merriam-webster.com/dictionary/restoration

Definitions

Meaning of the Name Giovanna
https://meaning-of-names.com/italian-names/giovanna.asp

Meaning of the Name George
https://meaning-of-names.com/english-names/george.asp

Saint George
https://en.wikipedia.org/wiki/Saint_George

Welcome to the truth
https://welcometotruth.com/blogs/apologetics/pro-life

ABOUT THE AUTHOR

Carolyn Booker Pierce is a licensed social worker, teacher, mentor, and spiritual leader born and raised in Columbus, Ohio.

After leaving a career of almost 20 years in accounts payable and claims auditing, Carolyn followed her passion in the area of social services. She then graduated with a BA at Capital University to become a licensed social worker. Carolyn gravitates to chemical dependency counseling as a substance abuse group and individual counselor.

Later she took her years of experience as a substance abuse counselor into her local county jail to serve inmates struggling with substance abuse, alcoholism, and family relationship problems. She is known for listening to others without judgment as they process their everyday life problems.

Carolyn desires to help people grow, heal from their past, and move on to a healthy future. She enjoys spending time with her family, church worship center, traveling, writing, and empowering others.

facebook.com/carolyn.pierce.5245

ALSO BY CAROLYN BOOKER-PIERCE

Because the Lord is My Shepherd: Psalm 23 and Me

Girl, You're Not Crazy. You're Dealing With a Narcissist

Loving the Addict: While Taking Care of Yourself First

www.ingramcontent.com/pod-product-compliance
Lightning Source LLC
Chambersburg PA
CBHW071507070526
44578CB00001B/470